Apostrophe

Apostrophe

—

Elizabeth Robinson

Apogee Press
Berkeley · California
2006

Acknowledgements

The author thanks the editors of the following periodicals in which some of these poems have appeared: *Alice Blue, The Canary, Conjunctions, Copper Nickel, Double Room, English Language Notes, Marginalia, No, One Less, Rooms, Small Town, Traverse.*

"The End of the World" also appeared as a limited print chapbook published in conjunction with the Left Hand Books Reading Series in Boulder, Colorado.

Many thanks to Ed Smallfield and Alice Jones for supporting my work. My particular and heartfelt thanks to Ed Smallfield, Valerie Coulton, Julie Carr, and Susanne Dyckman for insightful reading of this manuscript and invaluable friendship.

Apogee Press would like to thank Susanne Dyckman for her work on this book and for her contributions to the press.

Cover daguerreotype, "Unidentified elderly woman with cap," reprinted with permission of the Library of Congress.

Book design: Philip Krayna Design, Berkeley, CA.
www.pkdesign.net

ISBN 0-9744687-9-7. Library of Congress Card Number 2005937676.

Published by Apogee Press
Post Office Box 8177
Berkeley, CA 94707-8177
www.apogeepress.com

Table of Contents

...grace is not dependent on conditions of any kind and can lightly, at any point, reverse the chronology of a hundred years. It's independent of the sequential, evolutionary ways in which our earthly stories normally unfold. Thus grace, while it creates narratives where there were none, also creates unusual narrative structures...a story that turns on grace turns on an unprecedented factor that is inherently lawless and unpredictable...

—SUSANNAH LESSARD

The poem baldly asserts what is false: that a living hand, warm and capable, is being held toward us, that we can see it. The narrator contrasts his life with death, proleptically predicting that when he is dead the reader will seek to overcome his death, will blind himself to his death by an imaginative act. We fulfill this icy prediction...by losing our empirical lives: forgetting the temporality which supports them and trying to embrace a purely fictional time in which we can believe that the hand is really present and perpetually held toward us through the poem.

—JONATHAN CULLER

The Nocturnal Bridge

Under the field,
its flowing substance,

are gaps in the span—
        who parts

but lovers,
self from beloved self.

        Falling down:
        analogue to making a crossing.

        This is the ticket to
        the undercurrent.

        Twigs, dust, evening
        all stumble,

        mix air and movement
        into paste.

As though it were also

beneath itself,
foraging and awash—

the bridge
urging

to its trespass.

The beloved body interred

in the free black air.

Gift

You are to be wrapped securely,
to rest now, proffered.
The cover soothes itself
as it falls across your profile.

But the dream hand lifts ahead of you,

casting and castigating.

Why

this ill dream today
put in the midst of no sure thing.
Cast,

plaything, this is
weary's bauble
all undone:
stirring inside
in the trinket's clutch.

The End of the World

If the end of the world is coming soon, the last desire intends to measure its limited geography. To know where to find certain of its bodies, still animate, and where they lay.

The end will also follow sequence, but these bodies abstain from that pattern.

You know that I always approach you from behind. That is not because I'm furtive, but because I am afraid that a part of you might start up and run away if you saw me coming. I want to see you in your completeness. Because all bodies, animate or not, crave for something to be entire.

What eros most fears is not the end. Yet.
To partake of another world and believe that it would suffice.

That unbearable interpolation in endings.

You know that my faith is always and only most immediate.

Or if absurd belief turned to an alternate hope.

The wedge that comes in, that interrupts closure.

Though you continue to live at a remove, and that
is another thing interposed; we call it a reply.

We stand outside, shoulder to shoulder. Though shoulders
are figurative terms, and spacing is a matter of hankering, thirst, itch.

While distances are increasingly abbreviated.

So this is how we drink.

In this new and truncated world, it rains incessantly, and we are not allowed the tools of the household, only curve's edge.

That is, like creatures bereft. We put back our heads and expose our open mouths to precipitation.

And parts of us dislocate, like rangy animals, walk off to foresee the demise. That persona by which I self-describe

who would locate your shoulder, for leaning, or your unshut mouth, for receiving.

If the end of the world were put off indefinitely, then geography is delayed too. All obviousness bounces back on itself; the world is not resilient, but waiting has an elastic resemblance to the features of the body.

I am not, and never have been, interested in
the shape of the world whose decay affronts me,
but its function as a funnel or peephole onto the specific,
the strained relation of parts.

Geography as a sieve. Mouth hovering
under the curve it understands as cup. Globe about to burst.

If the edge of the world is forestalled, then we can continue to confuse intention with fulfillment. This is like an elbow or knee, the bending sample of a piecemeal body.

Mapping connective tissue amid the caress.

One of a pair throws, compactly, a narrative into yet another physiognomy and watches it unfurl like a stride.

I had wanted to inquire, and had waited this long to begin.

Doorway

This is the house of conviction
you come into.

Characters play here,
blurred, coming into

movement
made inside frame.

Passive hardware. The address
is resistless at its new site.

The characters crave their old positions. Once,

they stood, so,

on their parts. The frame of address

first laid upon.

And then implanted.

Where one finds oneself. The roof-peak,
the angle of wall to floor.

Where one finds oneself, one imagines,
is as one fell.

The characters that comprise a house
exist in this:

like weather falling down, you did
enter, the shape of the house bent aside.

The atmosphere is nailed together.
Limb marking threshold.

Each element struggles to
make threat subservient

to shelter.

Lost

i.

Direct is caressing direction,

is making her regret.

Flexed or embraced

depending on whose intention

was withstood or under

understood.

There was that gentle incline

inevitable

from A to B

the inside of the inside

whose ease makes one stumble

where there is no

finding one's way.

Behind or late,

tender to the hard

balance or on

her its malleable lack.

Wind

And you were wandering up the hill. One and two the days were,
wrapped in a fabric. Between us, we could estimate the spelling that
led from the days numbered to a sense of world. This wandering
made of fuzz and nap. Time takes objects and lays them flat. Then we
can feel the pelt, that material, underneath our disorientation.
My back pressed up against your back, and time's tensile in between.

I would rather have a lover than a doppelgänger. Confetti falls from the storm and adheres to this version as "world." There are improper spaces between us. Or perhaps it's just that the weather is foul, but it has its duty too.

Rifts in the continuity that make a human from a series. Time rolls out as a blanket accidentally, and protects us from the wind. One blanket underneath and one blanket on top, for the two made out of the interruption.

This wind once had shapely language, but we strayed and it conformed to us.

To stray is not so wrong, just a lost stitch. Or too much interest in needles: the tool should not overstep—the continuity between you and self. Wind is blowing by and that makes the string that someday ends with fabric. What spindle pricks. What aimless breeze knows its way beyond breath.

A further commitment to air.

If you went wandering upward, then the state of the world is by necessity tugged away from itself like a sail. That is: I kiss you tongue in my cheek. The redundance is all that gives, gives us elasticity.

You were the beloved in a gust. Some fleck returns to light on the flat world. Flat more precarious than round. Space which marks "tick-tock" also measures as chain mail, insuperable barrier. To be so accompanied and never to have touched the world, these matched parts that the mirror will refuse as lint.

Anemone

Feral and a garland,
who touches is cut.
And all about us, we equivocate:
dialogue, fretted petals. Affection
is a surround. See, the equation,

the obvious festoon. In the contingent moment
who will awake, just as the flowers warned.
I will wake an equation, always evasive.
And always particular, this futile adding

and dividing. The garland carries a message,
script writ bold in its loop. And then severed, mild anagram
of reverse. I cut a hole in 'hedge,' no matter what I've
transposed or who makes to surround what
no admonition can counter, and see–
how the image qualifies.

Lost

ii.

What is right
has never yet
yielded at its core
while the weight
gives onto her,
even asks

a balance wide
enough and quiet:
to imply
an escape
misplaced.

Be late

and that unforgiving

lateness

is the shape. To call her

flesh or balance or not

the way out of.

Alba: the *caracol*

Let undeclared

night delay

the past.

Nothing as arbitrary

as time can feign

song. Bereft

spiral.

Day

The day
rising from the floor

of time
throws shadows. Today's

violence
is familiar,

hinged as a door,
the fraud
of accessibility.

What you
in the day
are,
some vertical movement

meant to meet the gaze
and notched with passage.

Round Tower

I have a dream in which this sister explains
that otherwise than in the dream I would not

have known her. I take her to a round tower.
There, I put my hands in
her armpits and drag downward.

I put my mouth to her in her tower

she will take away.

We have an understanding, and peel its stucco
skin back, like bark from a birch.
What I can endow. I can smell it, a spiral

that bares itself. Underneath
a skin whose precision I prize above all. I see there

myself as lingering, indirect and patient.

If I were to wake up
in the obscure comfort of the bed, I could still smell it,

what she is saving from me. I had loved the

indirection of my prize. It seemed possible that
one could go on and not lose way. Like the birch,
the form seemed pliable.

Its internal shape stood in for no one. If I waited,

I could sustain love. I would be keen enough. I think
of dreamscapes as trite. But the drag of hands
over a flayed building seemed possible.

Anagram for Memory

Rumor, too,
is a kind of gravity.

How the light pulls,
pulls west

toward sunset's rearrangement.

How the shore cuts
preposterously
mid-continent,

its rumored earthquake.
All light

capped or memorialized.
Memory as idiolect,

incomprehension,
its arms bared in all light

toward the sleeveless errand.

The world can stretch
to mismatch and euphony

without redeeming the pull to ground.

Discarded Garments

The world made of soot produced these white things,
and look how they cling to form. We dug them up
with our darkened hands.

Inside the puzzle, we saw the sleeves fall back
where we protect arms that were ours. We did not question what
we'd touched. The interior has shed its dolorous husk, and the riddle
turned round to bathe us.

And so the compassion of the antonym:
the insoluble puzzle,
the light-bearing raiment, the hand who
flushes itself from the earth, reaching for us as its found garment.

Forward of this answer, what other
reclamation?
Fear, the gentle guide, accompanies us.
We tally the incongruous; we unearth.

Guessing at the Name

What we thought was done
bore its own backtracking
spine or filament

into new union.

As though
by whispering *straw*
in the heat of passion

we could spin

and spin.

Some golden absence magnified
requires a name.

The collision,
as we approached,
departed in ire

who are now so forsaken
on this steady thoroughfare.

What is the vehicle that
asks its name to leap
fully formed from its
own mouth.

The spine or byway dead ends
at a cliff
where we revolve downward
unknowing.

Ourobouros, come out
from your gold cocoon.

Put your mouth by mine and I will tell you
the name of your offspring.

We had known better to spin
the habiliments of the landscape
into

what precious
revision

and call it our relation.

Serpentine, child,
between itself and name.

We saw a wheel, turning in night,
toward transformation
on a crooked road.

Then returning
a favor is to
turn back on truth,

not that we couldn't tell
the creature his name
and reclaim our
heir,

but that a name is a place,
inhuman gold

soft on the palate
where we go aloud
in conjecture.

Letter (domino, elevation)

Dear Listener,
subsequent dominoes fall
and the one who betrays most
makes eye contact without otherwise heeding.

Dear,
what I depicted I saw only above
and did not know any other grasp
by which to detain.

Dear Elevation,
your sere layering
would have disarmed me
if I had not already
backtracked on my own.
My treachery is gentle on myself,

and high up.

I know that I was made by God
so that my head could rotate on its
angle and look up.
I do as I am told by the falling parade
of black, clacking disks
that tumble downward in disarray.

Dear One, and not Two,
how I have held you
with all my mind
and not my self, above.
My love for you refuses all it might,
gold and deaf.
High and away my eyes light upon
what they could have taken.

Radiant

quo animo?

These constellations
will fall

and the wave
over us

comes, light
toppled on itself.

What follows from
the ray,

but more

of itself

and so clustered,

the wave
doubled
over,

rigid,

we are made to
fall before

what we
happened upon.

In the beginning
was chaos,
the disorder who
absorbed color
and it embraced
the body,
that it was as it

was:
extending as from
a wheel,
divine
manufacture
implies no judgment.

Refractory in heat,

all happenstance
of light

falls here.

Wave or flame, undulate,

meant
to emit

forward

motion

in what
spirit—

In the beginning,

the self

could

comprehend

its own embrace

as felicitous

splitting,

the two of us

known

in tumult's

spare flame.

We ongoing
in its flaring.

The progressive
liquid
disturbance
we enclose
the beam
will
indicate.

The ray
retracted
would burn itself.

The entire purpose
of the constellations

was to die
and send this shower.

A stream of particles,

it is
upon us

this luminous body

moved straightaway.

From what
does dying
relieve
or ripple.

So the damned
understand
differently,
the flame's
wavering form
collapsing
the body
onto
the body,
into itself
abiding
onset.

If there was

a beginning,

this 'we'

as initiate,

                a unified pronoun, that—

      And outward moving

      this lack—

Grace will fall
too
from diurnal sky,

in what spirit

given or

sent,

if wave
and flame

know

they cannot go back.

Animate,

we so want

this rejoinder

to be begun.

The body

in us

instilled

in the body we

divine,

or divide

the motion to itself.

In what spirit
does fidelity
acquire longing?

Inexorable truth
loves motion.

The ray
loves its object
infinitely.

The spokes
formed on impact, these

are longing's

inveterate wheel.

So that
the spirit or fact
created to extend
endlessly from itself

may still
in such spirit
fall back
or roll forward
tender as it is
to its own redundance.

Anemone

petal: a combining form meaning "seeking"
used in the formation of compound words,
as "centripetal"—seeking or directed to
the center

I begin counting, and each number, as in '1,'
is a breath inflating your body, a body on a stem,

2 or 3, one of the segments of the corolla of a
flower. That is, the exhalation of the 4th color
deepens the body. A fifth petal secrets itself. Air is always
blue if seen from the distance that properly weds it.
Also branching from the stem, this aspirated
6, leaf, 7. Now I grow from you as from the

waist of the tilted 8, infinite, the mark of the infinite half.
An organic thing stretched 9 times, the pliancy
of the maximum tethered by stem to roots. Ten times deeper
than that, one by the side of one, soil can turn
its dozen tints to a bloodstained blue. Excavate;
an unlucky number; botanical abacus. My
sapphire number. Floret. Rales. Such as the lungs count.

Entrance

This particular passion
desires that all things be made small.

And for once the object
does not crash to the floor,

but miniaturized,
leaps up &

alights in your hand.

Your hands,
their fingers so elongated,

fold back to the compact palm.

Having so flown,

the desire
will compress.

To fit into your body as this does.

To take a fit.

To drink and so
to rage.

To achieve an ideally small
and avid state.

So to circle around your fingers
& ring them.

This tension between pronouns,
the manifest

movement
of fixation. Have I
not stilled upon
you.

Infuriating grasp
of the hand upon
its own shrinkage.
Buoyant, these slight
lips captured in the palm.
Smaller and smaller
as passion would have us
lisp.

There was a pattern
below these two selves
on which they trod.
Each path has its single dimension.

Each lover is the product of a neglectful lover.
Into your hand, it springs. I rise there.

Into your hand, held up as shield
to your breast.
I was the lover, or at least
not the other,
so diminished with rare love
as to infuse you.

　　　And not the reverse.
　　　What entrapment constitutes the self
　　　so that it does not leave?

Each beloved loves its other,
who might venerate the entrance.
To be entranced, captured,
ever littler,
the density of this riot
so bodily astute
as to find its way in,
r-pture.
To make off: spring
and welling up,
the
short exchange of vowels.

Arrow

If the arrow
hits its mark,
it breaks flesh.

Then the body
divides in two,
and the arrow
as well.

This is how
the world divides,

and the result of pain
is its secrecy. The two
bodies it creates:

a mouth around
a barb, and essential

that word
choked back.

The I adopts a verb
and becomes its lover.

Then arrows become
indicators

pointing at them
in their duress.

If there are now
two arrows

coming late to their
target, they see

the breaking of split
selves that ought

to have happened.

Where the body arcs
it waits and expects
to meet them.

One verb
in many tenses

traces the feather
on the arrow's tail

in all the bodies' motion.

Arrow
not divisible

from the sender
as the point of
its final contact.

To revise the body
by any means

from its solitary
habit,

this taking aim
and releasing.

Late and later
the air

compressing on motion

to deter

the arrow

from this recognition—

bouquet splaying
in air,

all possible motions

caught in the net
of the verb

swathing the body.
What word

can rise and incline

as target.
To injury

as it divides
give grasp.

Anemone

Cold and Aegean,
one blossom
supports entire
the blue it
purports. Block
of flower

built to a tower.
This height, recirculated,
deepens. Entangled
inside its own color.
Headlong the flower
throws itself from
its own precipice,
foreign to its fall.

Speak

Address is its own metaphysics. See: the
hereafter in which I speak, now, solely
in your voice.

Certain tunes tune themselves this way.
United, but how shall I ever know, speaking
in a voice that I would adopt from you.

Here is a book in which the both of us
believe in god. One reads from the front
and the other from the back.

So states the divine voice: that there
is a middle. Where is it that we do
not meet?

I speak in your voice to say that what
I heard once is also what I said, that there
is a word drawn out, something less than faith,

and where, I do not know, but that a thing I
desire could extend from me. Willful religion:
that a voice could have its impact.

I carried close my small transcendent, like
a balm, but I have your voice now. The
mutual god is all immanent, the center

that dispenses with pronouns.

PHOTO: Linnea Lenkus

ELIZABETH ROBINSON was educated at Bard College, Brown University, and Pacific School of Religion. She is now on the creative writing faculty at the University of Colorado, Boulder. Her previous books include *In the Sequence of Falling Things, Bed of Lists, House Made of Silver,* and *Harrow.* She won the National Poetry Series for *Pure Descent* and was the winner of the Fence Modern Poets Series for *Apprehend.* She co-edits EtherDome Press, *26 Magazine,* and Instance Press.

Other Poetry Titles from Apogee Press

Among the Names
Maxine Chernoff
"This book is entirely
beautiful."
—Donald Revell

passing world pictures
Valerie Coulton
"Swift and rich, an entire
world passes here
in vivid glimpses."
—Cole Swensen

In the absent everyday
Tsering Wangmo Dhompa
"A terrific poet, on any
terms."
—Ron Silliman

Rules of the House
Tsering Wangmo Dhompa
"A lovely explication of 'dhar-
ma'—things as they are,
and how precious they are."
—Anne Waldman

Discrete Categories Forced
into Coupling
Kathleen Fraser
"I love Fraser's extraordinary
intelligence, her persistent
care for where she is."
—Robert Creeley

Gorgeous Mourning
Alice Jones
"Dazzling poems, wholly
taken in by where the words
are going." —Adam Phillips.

cloudlife
Stefanie Marlis
"Aphoristic, enigmatic, and
startling."—C.D. Wright

fine
Stefanie Marlis
"An etymology of our sexual
and physical lives, our
unknown lives, our daily
lives." — Edward
Kleinschmidt Mayes

Speed of Life
Edward Kleinschmidt Mayes
"These poems are at the
harsh center of things."
—Eavan Boland

bk of (h)rs
Pattie McCarthy
"This is simply a gorgeous
book." —Cole Swensen

Verso
Pattie McCarthy
"One of our most intellectual-
ly ambitious poets."
—Ron Silliman

Human Forest
Denise Newman
"Like imbibing a divine elixir,
making one
realize how thirsty one has
been all this time."
—Gillian Conoley

Apprehend
Elizabeth Robinson
"I feel a securing confidence
in her poems—as if she had
given me her hand."
—Robert Creeley

The Pleasures of C
Edward Smallfield
"These are poems of thrilling
uneasiness and probing
reward." —Kathleen Fraser

Oh
Cole Swensen
"*Oh* is opera cool."
—Marjorie Perloff

dust and conscience
Truong Tran
"Something important is
going on, something
wonderful."—Lyn Hejinian

placing the accents
Truong Tran
"To be entered, and entered.
Gratefully." —Kathleen Fraser

within the margin
Truong Tran
"Truong's masterwork
delivers a 'meteor storm.'"
—Juan Felipe Herrera

**To order, or for more
information go to
www.apogeepress.com**